This Notebook Belongs To

Quick Note

Printed in Great Britain
by Amazon

60447890R00070